A BABY OF OUR OWN,

A NEW BABY IN A STEPFAMILY

by Erica De'Ath

Published by

STEPFAMILY
Publications
THE NATIONAL STEPFAMILY ASSOCIATION

© NATIONAL STEPFAMILY ASSOCIATION, October 1993

ISBN 1 873309 10 4

All rights reserved. No part of this publication may be reproduced, stored in a retrieval system, or transmitted in any form or by any means, electronic, mechanical, photocopying, recording or otherwise without the prior permission of the publisher.

Published by

STEPFAMILY Publications
National Stepfamily Association
72 Willesden Lane,
London NW6 7TA, England.

Telephone
071 372 0844 (office) 071 372 0846 (counselling helpline)

Registered Charity No 1005351
Company Limited by guarantee 2552166

Printed by Lonsdale Press Ltd
Designed in house by STEPFAMILY
Illustrations from NCVS & Caroline Firenza, The Drawings Pack
Cover illustration from NCVS & Caroline Firenza, The Drawings Pack

ACKNOWLEDGMENTS

We are very grateful to a number of people who gave detailed advice and comments on early drafts of this booklet, especially Mary Newburn, Mary Anne Crook, Mary Daly, Donna Smith and Jacquie Reed.

Particular thanks are due to June Mason who wrote the first publication for STEPFAMILY on 'A Baby of Our Own' in 1986.

The issues covered in this revised and expanded booklet show how varied and complex it can be to live in a stepfamily. Thank you to all those who contributed their own story. Thank you also to those who read and commented on the manuscript, again often drawing on their own personal as well as their professional experience.

We are delighted that the Health Visitors Association are endorsing this booklet. They are probably the best placed to offer sensitive and appropriate advice and support to those struggling with some of the dilemmas we have outlined. They can also share in the joy of all the stepfamily members watching the new child of the stepfamily grow up.

Finally, our thanks go to the National Council for Voluntary Child Care Organisations who contributed to the funding of this booklet through the Department of Health's small grants scheme.

STEPFAMILY is the only national organisation providing support, advice and information for all members of stepfamilies and those who work with them. There are local contacts and groups in Northern Ireland, Scotland, Wales and England.

STEPFAMILY AIMS TO:

promote a changing image of family life
support practical step-parenting
encourage research into and information on remarriage and stepfamily life
provide training materials and opportunities for those working with stepfamilies

STEPFAMILY OFFERS A WIDE RANGE OF SERVICES TO MEMBERS:

confidential telephone counselling
2 newsletters:
STEPFAMILY for adults
STEPLADDER for children
local support groups
information packs, books and leaflets
conferences, seminars and training workshops

membership is open to all who wish to support our aims above.

For further information contact:
STEPFAMILY, 72 Willesden Lane, London, NW6 7TA
Telephone:
071 372 0844 (Office) 071 372 0846 (Helpline)

ANNUAL MEMBERSHIP AT 1993

£15.00 for an individual £20.00 for couples
£30.00 for Associate Membership
(professional, voluntary or statutory bodies)

Registered Charity No. 1005351
Company Limited by guarantee 2552166

CONTENTS

Introduction	7
What is a stepfamily?	9
Should we have a baby of our own?	9
Trying to decide	11
Am I too old?	
Can we afford it?	
Do we have room?	
How do we involve everyone in the stepfamily?	
Deciding not to have a child	15
Medical matters	
Past experiences	
A couple, not parents	
Existing children	
Childlessness	18
Deciding to have a child	20
Uniting the stepfamily	
Disrupting the stepfamily	
Having the best of both worlds	
Race, culture and faith	
Will I love my own child more?	
A new baby in the stepfamily	25
Pregnancy and birth	
After the birth	
Being at home with the baby	

New roles and responsibilities for family members		30
    Stepfather as father
    Stepmother as mother
    Mother, stepmother and new mother
    Children and stepchildren
    A new baby for mother and for daughter
    Grandparents and grandchildren

New families, new babies, new hopes		43

Useful books		46

Useful addresses		47

INTRODUCTION

Every year thousands of babies are born into a stepfamily, bringing a half-brother or half-sister to all the other children in the stepfamily. Over half (52%) of all full-time stepfamilies have at least one joint child and probably the same number of part-time stepfamilies also have children of the new couple.

Stepfamilies often have to juggle lots of competing demands. Some stepchildren may be living in the home all the time and others visit at weekends or holidays. With children often moving between two homes family life can seem quite noisy and disruptive at times. Stepfamilies are often big families, four or five children is not unusual, so a new baby might seem just one more too many or too costly!

This booklet is for those stepfamilies who are thinking of having a child of their own. Although many people say 'we will just wait and see what happens and cope with it when we need to', we hope the experiences of others will give you an idea of some of the things to consider. We also hope it will help avoid some difficulties and misunderstandings that can occur if you are unclear as a couple whether you want a baby or not.

This booklet is also for those who already have a new baby and are seeking some help and tips on coping with some of the issues that may have arisen. A baby can be a bundle of joy one minute and screaming its head off the next. We hope to guide you through the undoubted happiness and togetherness that a baby can bring to a stepfamily without skirting over the intense jealousy, guilt and disappointment that can also arise.

We hope it will help you to make your decision, to prepare for the baby if that is your choice, and to understand the variety of ways different members of the stepfamily may react to any new addition.

Being a parent is hard work with many responsibilities. Being a parent and a step-parent at the same time can be doubly hard but also doubly rewarding.

Erica De'Ath *Margaret Buttigieg*
National Stepfamily Association Health Visitors Association
October 1993

WHAT IS A STEPFAMILY?

As a stepfamily one of you, or perhaps both of you, already have a child or children from a previous relationship. The children may live with you and your partner or they may stay over at weekends or holidays, or just visit occasionally. A stepfamily may bring together adults and children with different experiences of how a family works. Children learn that rules and traditions can vary when they visit the homes of their school friends, but it can be more difficult living with such differences. In a stepfamily some children may move on a regular basis between two homes with different expectations about how they should behave.

Most stepchildren have had to cope with the loss of one of their parents. For some the loss is that they no longer live together in the same house but still see each other regularly. For others, the loss is greater and there may be only occasional visits. For many children there is no contact at all with their absent parent who is often their father. And for a few, their parent has died and so there is no hope of seeing them ever again. How children coped with such loss and how they feel about losing important people in their childhood can often play a very important part in how they adjust to new people coming into their lives.

SHOULD WE HAVE A BABY OF OUR OWN?

Most couples usually ask themselves this question at some point in their relationship. The issues will usually be about whether they want children at all, and if so when. A stepfamily is slightly different in that at least one of you already has a child, so there may be mixed emotions and conflicting feelings. For one of you it may be a question of whether to have a first child while for the other it is whether to have another child.

A childless stepmother may think that stepchildren can be a substitute for having her own child but then finds she longs for her own child. A separated father may be torn between his financial responsibilities to his first children, his respect for his wife's decision not to have another child or to maintain her career, but he may

long for the day to day fathering of children with his new wife. A couple both with their own children may feel a deep urge to have their own joint child as a central commitment within the stepfamily.

Couples in stepfamilies sometimes ask themselves this question as part of exploring their relationship, rather than as a serious intention to have a child. What would it have been like if we had met when we were younger? If this had been our first marriage? What kind of parents would we have been together? What would our child have been like? Would it be different looking after a child who is ours alone compared to one who is a stepchild? What qualities would our child have that might be different to existing children in the stepfamily?

> *Parents at forty or a dream baby?*
> *Ross and Annie have both been married before with two children each who all live with them. They have talked on and off over the last three years about having their own baby and their teenage children are bored with it. Annie is 43 years old and believes that she still could have a baby if she wanted to. She finds the thought of sleepless nights and the fact that she would be sixty when the baby was the same age as her eldest boy now, shocks her back into practical reality.*
>
> *'No way do I really want one, but I like the idea of us having a child. It's my dream baby of what might have been but it doesn't get in the way of my real life with either my kids or Ross's. When we first talked of having a baby all the children were shocked, then they giggled. We told them we both loved them all as children and as stepchildren and it was only natural we should think about what it might have been like if we'd have one together. That seemed to make sense to them.'*

Most couples talk about having their own child at some point in a committed relationship as it is such a visible sign of their committal to each other both now

and in the future. Many couples decide a child is a very important part of that relationship and the building of their own family. For others it may be something they would like to have done but decided for a whole variety of reasons not to put into practice. This happens in first marriages as well as second or subsequent ones.

TRYING TO DECIDE

Having a baby is a big step and in a stepfamily there are many other people who will be affected by your decision and your actions. It is understandable that many people say 'we will just wait and see what happens and cope with it when we need to.' Talking to others can undoubtedly help, but it is not always easy to find someone in a similar position to yourself.

At each annual STEPFAMILY members conference there is always a group of men and women who want to discuss having a baby of their own. Often there is a difference of opinion between the couple. (One wishing to have a baby whilst the other does not, or being very dubious about the impact on their relationship as well as on the children and the stepfamily as a whole.) Stepfamily members have frequently told researchers how precarious stepfamily life can be. There is a worry that any change, especially a baby, could tip the balance from harmony into chaos, from a delicate truce to outright warfare!

We hope the many case studies that run through this booklet will reassure you that you are not alone in struggling with some of these conflicting emotions and anxieties. We have identified some specific things to consider and hope it will help avoid some difficulties and misunderstandings that can occur if either of you is unsure whether you want a baby. If you do want a baby, how would you cope when one comes? Or equally important, how will you cope if you discover you cannot conceive?

Am I too old?

One of you may feel too old to start a second family. This is not the same as being too old! Many women in their late thirties and early forties are having children. While late pregnancies may require extra care they are no longer considered to be such a risk as in the past. As an older parent you may have more maturity and experience of life and, perhaps, more patience than when you were in your early twenties.

Fathers often say they feel they missed out on a great deal of their children's early years. Many were too busy working long hours to establish their career and earning the extra money needed to finance a family. This second chance to enjoy fatherhood, when men are in their forties or fifties, in a more relaxed and involved way, may be one of the reasons that the older children feel resentful and cheated at the attention given by their father to a new half-brother or sister.

Some may feel rejuvenated by parenthood, others may be overwhelmed by the constraints of age. Anxieties about health and whether you will be able to deal with the physical stress of looking after a new baby is something you need to discuss together, and with your family doctor or health visitor. You may be concerned about a child growing up with elderly parents and how you will meet the additional costs as you near retirement. If you have good relationships with other family members it would be good to discuss it with them as well if you are planning to call on them for help.

Can we afford it?

Stepfamilies often find that their finances are not theirs alone to control. It will be important to sit down and work out calmly:

* how much money is coming into the stepfamily?
* how much money is going out?
* how much do you currently need to support the family?
* will one of you have to give up work to look after a baby?
* if you plan to arrange child care, how much will it cost?

* what will you need as a family with a new baby?
* are there likely to be extra costs for existing children in the stepfamily?
* are there likely to be any changes in any of the child support payments?
* are either of you likely to have additional expenses for elderly parents?
* how would you cope with redundancy or early retirement?

Remember most couples and families find their income strained by the arrival of a child.

If you or your partner have financial obligations from a previous relationship it will be essential to consider whether these are likely to change over the next five to ten years and discuss this with the ex-partner if at all possible.

If you are both working, you will need to consider whether the woman's job allows for maternity leave. Will she qualify for maternity benefit? Could the stepfamily manage on one wage in the months following the birth? Would any child support payments become a problem, either coming into or going out of the stepfamily?

If you are struggling with any of these questions then you can seek advice and assistance from your local Citizen's Advice Bureau. The Child Support Agency has a formula for working out child support that came into effect from 5 April 1993. If you need to apply for Family Credit or need a review or assessment of your child support payments, and if it is critical to your family income level, you should explore this before you make any decisions .

Do we have room?

All couples need to think about this, but in a stepfamily there are other questions to ask. As a stepfamily are you living in your own home or did one of you move into the previous family home? If so, will you need to re-arrange the bedrooms of the children or stepchildren and will this cause a problem? Whilst children often

have to move around in a family to make way for a new baby, stepchildren may be less willing to move for a half-brother or sister and may see them as an intruder in their family and home.

If you have already decided that you would need to move, then do think of the needs of your children and stepchildren as well as the new baby. Would a move make it more difficult for them to visit their other parent? Or for visiting children to come and stay with you? Can you actually afford to move?

How do we involve everyone in the stepfamily?
If at all possible let your children know of your decision to have a baby before you conceive. This gives them a chance to get used to the idea and to express negative feelings before you celebrate becoming pregnant. Once a pregnancy is confirmed a family discussion is definitely a good idea, so that everyone knows of the forthcoming event. Children and stepchildren, as well as grandparents and step-grandparents, are often very hurt to discover this kind of information from other people. In some stepfamilies it may be better to talk to children individually as their reactions may be very different and they may not be supported by their siblings. You will know your children best. It may be helpful if both the parent and step-parent talk to each child on separate occasions. Encouraging everyone to be involved is one way of trying to avoid anyone feeling excluded.

It is particularly important to discuss such an important event with all the children in the stepfamily. Do not put them in the position where they think they are making the decision. Seek their views, try and unravel what their anxieties and concerns are beforehand so you can be aware and reassure them. Remember that children are often concerned about really simple practical matters:

* where will the baby sleep?
* will they have to share their bedroom with the baby?
* will they have to move out of their room?
* will they have to share with someone else in the stepfamily?
* can they still have their friends around, and play their music?

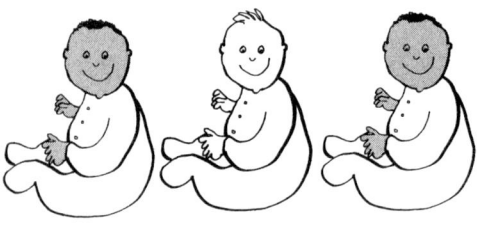

* will there still be time for them with their own parent?
* will their parent still love them as much?
* will there still be money for new clothes and family holidays?
* will their step-parent love them at all if they have their own child?
* will they be expected to baby-sit for you when they come to stay?
* will resident stepchildren have to baby-sit regularly, will they get paid?

Only you as the parent and step-parent can make the decision about whether to have a baby. When you have done so, you then have a responsibility to your existing children and stepchildren to explain what your plans are and what changes might or will take place.

DECIDING NOT TO HAVE A CHILD

There are many couples today choosing not to have a child. There are many stepfamilies choosing not to add any more children to a ready-made stepfamily. Reasons will vary enormously but one of the most common factors is age, of both the adults and children! But there can be other reasons, such as a medical condition or past experiences which can influence such decisions.

Medical matters

If either of you has had a vasectomy or sterilisation, you can seek advice from your family doctor about the possibilities to reverse this situation. If there is a health risk or a bad experience in previous pregnancies it is important that you and your partner discuss this. As in all families, being honest about your own feelings and aware of your partners feelings is very important. By not sharing these matters with your partner you may be in danger of creating a problem. Saying you don't want more children could make your partner feel his/her wishes are not important. Or he or she may think you do not feel strongly enough about the new

family to want to have a joint child. If the reasons for not having a child are actually different then it may be helpful to seek counselling, as well as medical advice, as a couple to come to terms with this.

Past experiences

There may be very strong reasons why one of you is anxious about having a baby. Perhaps the anxiety, emotional disruption or financial responsibilities are too frightening. Maybe an event many years ago, such as an abortion, a miscarriage, stillbirth or cot death or post-natal depression makes you fearful of trying again. It is better to share these concerns and talk them through than hold yourself back and cut off your partner from those feelings and anxieties from the past.

A couple not parents

Where one partner has grown-up children and the other teenagers, you may feel that your relationship is based on being a couple rather than being parents. You may well have the responsibilities for your own and each other's children but you did not base your relationship on creating a new family through having children together. Couples, such as Ross and Annie, may flirt with the idea of a 'joint' child but there is an open and honest shared commitment and understanding that, in reality, there is no intention of having more children.

Existing children

The number and ages of children already in the stepfamily can also be a deciding factor for very different reasons. If there are already pressures within the stepfamily, a couple may reluctantly decide against having a new baby because they cannot imagine coping with yet another child.

> *Five children all under seven years old*
>
> *Rebecca has three children by her first marriage, aged 6, 4 and 2 years old. Her husband, Tom, has two children who live with them as their mother is dead. Tom's children are 3 years and eighteen months old. Rebecca is finding it extremely difficult to cope alone with so many children who are all so young.*

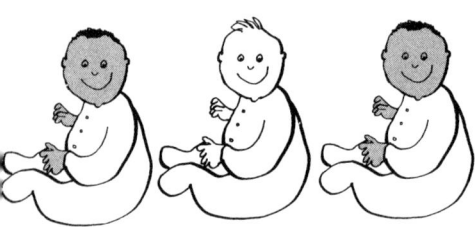

Although they would dearly love to have a child of their own and they have a supportive health visitor and Home Start befriender, they are frightened of the extra pressures a new baby might bring.

Younger children in the stepfamily may find it easier to adapt and the effect of a new baby may be very little different to that in any other family. Most child and baby care books have whole chapters devoted to introducing a new baby into the family and the effect a new arrival may have on other small children in the family. Research studies have indicated that most siblings do feel some jealousy at some point when a new baby arrives. Research also shows that parents and stepparents talking openly about the new baby and encouraging the other children to share any concerns and anxieties they have in the arrival of this new family member is actually more important in how a child will cope than their age, their position in the family or whether it is a stepfamily or not. Of course, each child in a family is different and may need different amounts of reassurance and involvement.

Older children may express their feelings more readily and appear resentful and pushed out. They may be afraid their own parent will be entirely absorbed in the new child and no longer have any interest in them. They may worry particularly about their own specialness with their parent - the only girl or boy, or losing their role as the youngest, as in the following example.

My Dad wants a baby!
After nearly twenty years of just having two daughters and telling us repeatedly that there would never be any more, my Dad told us he wanted to have another child. I began to feel spiteful. We were Dad's daughters. Nobody else. A boy would be bad enough - but a girl! I burst into tears at the thought of it.

It is worth bearing in mind that many of the reasons for not having a baby in a stepfamily will be the same for couples in a first family - lack of adequate

housing, lack of money, a life-style as a couple rather than as parents.

What is sometimes, but not always, different is the strained relationships that can exist within a stepfamily because of the difficulties of combining two families into one new household. Or the unsettled nature of family life because there are two sets of children moving between three different households. These are all good reasons for thinking carefully about how you all would cope. Since stepfamilies often combine two families where there are two or more children, the resulting family may already be quite large with four or five children. Whether a new child is a unifying factor or gets lost in the crowd is one of many challenges which face stepfamilies.

It is not surprising that many couples do feel the need to have something of their own, something which is not part of a previous relationship or someone else's family. A different decision - and this is a serious suggestion - may be to have a puppy or other pet. An animal can also be a focus for love and attention which helps to unite all members of a stepfamily and symbolise the new family and the new household.

CHILDLESSNESS

Coming to terms with not having a child may be more difficult for the step-parent who has never had a child. Having to accept your own childlessness with the constant reminder of your partner's children by someone else can be a stressful situation. This can be a painful and demanding role for both stepmothers and stepfathers and it is not necessarily any easier whether the stepchildren live with you all the time or not.

> *Accepting reality*
> *Pete and Sally had both been married before. Pete had three sons but Sally had no children. They had met at work and continued their married life as a working couple. After a few years Sally felt very strongly that she wanted a child with Pete.*

Sadly after many years of trying, seeking help and advice from numerous specialists they found that they would not have a child of their own. Pete tried to be sympathetic to Sally's deep disappointment but realised that he could never fully understand the loss of her dream or of her fulfilment of being a mother and a parent. He was still a very active parent to his sons. He would have liked another child with Sally but it was not so crucial to him as a husband or father.

No matter how committed and keen you are, there are couples who, despite everything, are unable to conceive a baby. This can be especially hard if you have discussed the matter at great length, prepared the other children in the stepfamily, and looked forward to the new dimension that a baby will bring to your stepfamily. It is hard not to feel angry and disappointed. There may be times when you resent others around you who appear to be able to conceive more readily. You may even have moments of resenting the other children. At such times it is important to seek some help either by phoning the STEPFAMILY Helpline or contacting other women or step-parents who may be in a similar situation.

It is just not fair!
Wendy got married at 35 and gave up her full-time job to prepare for motherhood. Her two stepsons came every other weekend and she enjoyed their company but she yearned for her own child. She wanted her stepsons to keep their strong relationship with their father and talked to them about how they could help her when she and their father had a baby. Unfortunately, years went by before Wendy became pregnant. During that time she found it very difficult to cope with her stepsons who resented the arrival of first one and then another baby in their other stepfamily. Wendy felt their mother and stepfather had not prepared the boys in the way she had tried to do and moreover they had two babies and she had none!

Over the years the smouldering resentment had created difficulties for her husband, her stepsons and the relationship between the two families.

It can take a great deal of love, patience and understanding from the partner who has children to acknowledge and support their partner through the natural feelings of resentment, jealousy, guilt and failure which may occasionally come in waves and overwhelm the partner who cannot have children.

DECIDING TO HAVE A CHILD

Many couples, both in families and stepfamilies, do not actually plan to have a child. At the same time, they are not planning not to have a child! Often this is because they are not sure whether they are ready for a child, or if they already have children whether they can cope with another so they 'leave it to nature'. When a pregnancy comes along they are delighted and start planning from there. Some couples do plan a pregnancy very carefully and others do not. Whilst one couple may be horrified at an accidental pregnancy, another would not have missed such a 'happy surprise'. For many, but not all couples, there is a feeling that to have a child with their partner is the ultimate commitment to their relationship.

Couples in stepfamilies who have planned a child do seem to be more aware of the potential problems. Even so, the reactions of family members may come as a shock. This will be discussed again later. When you've made your decision you need to work out who are the important people to include from the beginning, such as your children and stepchildren. How are you going to convey your continuing love and concern for them so that a baby will unite the stepfamily rather than disrupt it?

Grandparents and step-grandparents as well as uncles and aunts, sometimes feel the arrival of a baby in a stepfamily excludes them. Often they simply don't know how to react and may appear hostile when they are not. The reaction of an ex-

partner is the most difficult to assess and to handle. If the relationship is reasonably good, telling an ex-partner about an expected baby in the new family may help the children in their adjustment. If the relationship is tense and still full of conflict, the matter may be best handled through another family member.

Uniting the stepfamily

Some couples have said that a child in a stepfamily is a 'special' child. A child that will belong to everyone in the stepfamily. You and your partner will have created a child who will be more than just your child. He or she will also become a half-brother or sister to your children and your stepchildren, forming a tangible link between all the children and you as parents.

> *Strengthening the stepfamily*
>
> *Jim is 26 and married to Susan who has two boys, aged 6 and 9. They have just had a baby of their own, now aged 4 months. Jim is an extremely proud father and thinks the baby has united them as a family unit. He would rather they were a 'traditional' family than a stepfamily and is struggling to balance the two similar but very different roles of father and stepfather. He has started to question whether the boys should be seeing their father as frequently as every fortnight as he thinks this disrupts his relationship as their new father figure.*

A new baby can unite the stepfamily. At the same time a new baby can disrupt relationships between you and your stepchildren and between your stepchildren and their own absent parent. Stepfathers often become more possessive and protective of their stepchildren when they have become fathers themselves, particularly if their stepchildren are very young.

Disrupting the stepfamily

There are other ways in which a baby may disrupt a stepfamily. A mother or stepmother may be anxious about losing part of her independence if she has to stop working and be at home full-time with a baby again. There may be a loss of

income which would affect the household budget and child support payments.

Cementing a marriage
Mike and Nancy agreed they had enough children when they got married and she enjoyed the freedom they had as a couple now the children were older. Then Mike began to feel that a child of their own would bind them together more. Nancy felt this would disrupt their relationship rather than bring them closer.

If there are difficulties between you as a couple it is better to seek advice and counselling rather than believe that a new baby will resolve the matter.

An ex-partner may also find the arrival of a new baby disruptive and threatening. It is not unusual for there to be a revival of animosity. Having a baby is an extremely emotional experience and many ex-partners are amazed and sometimes alarmed at the strength of their feelings when they hear their ex-partner has had another child. Sometimes they are jealous, sometimes they are concerned that attention may be focused away from their children to the new baby, sometimes it just awakens buried feelings of anger, guilt, sadness, betrayal, loss and disappointment.

Several stepfamilies have been in touch with us describing the impact of a new baby within their stepfamily. Their experiences have been used throughout this booklet to let you know you are not alone. Because stepfamilies are so varied you will probably find that some of the issues and mixed feelings are ones you can identify with and others may seem strange. It is important to remember that when you talk to others, even other stepfamily members, each person will bring their own memories and very personal experiences. There are so many people involved in a stepfamily that it is hard for someone not to feel left out or uncomfortable at some point.

> ### *Flung into parenthood*
> *Angela wrote to tell us that her baby was just six weeks old when her partner was suddenly given his son by the boy's mother after a separation of two years. During that time he had seen his father only rarely and she had met the child only once. She has had to adjust to being a first-time parent with a new baby and to look after an active four year old uprooted from his home who has coped with a lot of different changes already in his childhood.*

This is a particularly dramatic response from an ex-partner who may have felt very jealous and angry at the thought of her ex-husband having a new family. It makes it harder for the stepmother and stepchild to form a positive relationship with each other when they are flung together in this way and a new baby could make it either easier for the little boy to be absorbed into the new stepfamily or more difficult because the stepmother is torn between her two very new roles and responsibilities.

Having the best of both worlds

One advantage of having another baby in a stepfamily is that you already have your past experience to draw upon. You may be more settled and secure in your home life in your thirties and forties than when you were in your teens or twenties.

> ### *Putting things into perspective*
> *Mary had two sons in her teens and two more in her thirties after her remarriage. She says that the babies brought a really important extra dimension to their lives. She thought she and her husband were better parents to her adolescent sons because with a demanding toddler and a new baby they can't become too preoccupied with the issues which many of their friends' parents are obsessed with such, as drugs and drinking and HIV.*

When you have your children close together it can make you very focused on one stage, whereas a big gap forces you to put things into a wider perspective and acknowledge the very different needs of children of such varied ages. It is also a wonderful opportunity for young people to understand the daily responsibilities of being a parent and to gain some practice with younger children before becoming parents themselves.

Race, culture and faith

Relationships between couples of different beliefs and races raise issues which need to be looked at sensitively as they can affect stepfamilies. A new baby may provide an opportunity to discuss such differences and how the many people related to the stepfamily may feel, react and cope with this. A new baby in any mixed-race or mixed-faith relationship can highlight the differences not only between the parents but also other family members. In a stepfamily this may create a particular difficulty if neither the parent or step-parent share the child's culture or beliefs. Equally the festivals, religious rites and family celebrations observed around the new baby may be different from those that the older children are familiar with. If they are told that the new baby must be accepted into a particular religion in order to have a place in heaven, and they are not member of that religion themselves, they may be both confused and distressed. It will be important, in such circumstances to anticipate such situations and agree as a couple how you handle their questions and concerns. There may be very particular issues for a stepchild of mixed race living in an otherwise all-white or all-black stepfamily, or for children who celebrate different religious festivals.

> *Some differences matter*
>
> *Judith (black) and Martin (white) were married for eight years and had one child, Sophie, who was five when her mother sadly died of cancer. Three years later Martin remarried. His new partner Pamela (white) had two children Robert (3) and Penny (5), from a previous relationship. Soon after she and Martin married she became pregnant with their son Jason.*

After Jason was born it became increasingly difficult for Pamela to hide her real feelings about Sophie.

'She's just so different from all of us. Everything about her is different. I can never do anything with her hair. It's always such a tangled mess and Martin's always going on about how I should use some kind of hair oil on it. And after she has her bath her skin gets these dry patches and he says I should rub some cream on, but I think he's making too much of a fuss over her. She even has to eat different food, and Martin sometimes brings her some terrible-smelling food from a West Indian takeaway shop he passes on the way home. None of my children get that sort of attention, not even the baby!'

Will I love my own child more?

Most parents want to do their best for all the children in their stepfamily. All parents have a range of feelings, emotions and love for their children. Each child is different and unique. The love you feel for your own child will almost certainly be different from that love which you feel for a stepchild. The love for a stepchild grows slowly over time and does not begin at the moment the child enters your life. That doesn't neccessarily mean you love any one child more or less than another but that you have different kinds of feelings and intensities of love for different people.

A NEW BABY IN THE STEPFAMILY

Talking about a baby is one thing, the actual arrival another. Remember, most people in a stepfamily have already experienced some major changes and upheavals in their life. Separation, divorce or death will have brought them into the stepfamily. Some of the children may have spent some time as a lone parent family and developed a very close relationship with that parent. The children may feel very threatened by a new baby, another competitor for their parent's time and

attention, no matter how much you have tried to reassure them.

Stepfamilies bring together two families which can be a complex set of relationships with some members getting on well and others not. Reactions to any baby can vary from family to family and within families. It is unrealistic to assume that:

* all the relatives will be as happy as the couple themselves
* once the baby arrives everything will work itself out.

Some simple planning, lots of discussion and awareness of the different feelings of all those involved is likely to make it easier.

Pregnancy and birth

A wide range of written material and parent magazines is available to inform future parents of what lies ahead and what you may encounter during pregnancy, labour, birth and the first few months of parenthood. Ante-natal classes, health visitors, midwives and family doctors are all there to offer help and advice where it is needed. However, they may not be aware and sensitive to the needs of stepfamilies and it will probably be up to you to raise any issues of concern. Their notes will be strictly related to the mother's parental status and they will assume it is a first, a second or a third baby for both of you! They may not realise that whilst this is a second baby you are a first-time father and so you may miss out on the information and reassurance given to other first-time fathers.

Couples are encouraged to make their own choices about maternity care, including whether the father is present at the birth and whether you want a home birth or hospital delivery. Having your partner present during labour can help you through a sometimes slow and uncomfortable process and can enhance your relationship as well as sharing the excitement, joy and tears of happiness at the moment of birth. This is a point where a stepfamily couple differs from first family couples. It may be a first birth for you as a couple but it will not be the first birth for at least one of you.

If as a father you did not attend the birth of your other children you may be reluctant to do so now. Perhaps you are genuinely frightened you could not cope, or feel that if you were going to be there you should have done it the first time around. Alternatively, your partner may have attended a birth before and found that he was not happy and does not want to repeat the experience. He may see no reason to be there.

Stepmothers who have already experienced childbirth may be quite happy to have the baby alone and be more concerned that you will take care of the rest of the children in the stepfamily. However, a stepmother who has not had children may be very anxious to have you with her and resent it if you are not present at the birth of your child. This may be especially so if you are absent to look after your children from your first family.

Fathers who attend the birth of their offspring often say they have an especially strong paternal feeling towards them. Being there may make a difference for some couples.

You will need to talk it out between you: how you feel, what you want to do at this special and sensitive time. You will need to try to understand each other's point of view. It may not be easy but, if you each want something different, it is worth sorting out and coming to an agreeable compromise. It may be very important to have your partner present at the birth, so every effort should be made to ensure that child care arrangements for the other children does not create an obstacle. Friends or grandparents may be able to help here.

After the birth
You may find after the birth how different you are from other couples with their first new baby. They will not have to cope with two children all week and four or five at the weekend, or a houseful for one month during holidays and none at all for the next three. Couples in a stepfamily never follow the simpler family progression from couple, to couple plus baby which expands to a family!

You may find that you have different attitudes, experiences, or expectations. A first-time mother or father may feel under pressure to compete with and perform better than a previous partner with breast or bottle feeding or coping with night feeds.

Having a baby is a tiring business. Like all couples it helps if you can arrange some extra help with the housework. This is always important in any family where there are other children. Parents need to spend time with all the children to reassure them they are all important. In a stepfamily some time must also be protected to allow you to be a couple on your own, as well as time with your new baby, without any of the children feeling excluded. This is not easy.

Having said all this - Don't always assume that any problems you have are because you are a stepfamily

Most children feel some jealousy when a new baby arrives in a family. It is well worth reading what the baby care books say about handling jealousy in other children.

Being at home with the baby

Hopefully, everyone in the stepfamily will have aired their concerns, worked out the differences and adapted to each other before the baby arrives. However, none of us are perfect and events rarely run totally to plan. People make mistakes and sometimes say things in the heat of the moment especially when they are tired.

We don't always do things the most appropriate way and misunderstandings can arise. You may be surprised at your and others emotional reactions. When the baby is actually there, jealousy and resentment may begin to show themselves. It may be that each of you had not fully realised how much change a new baby could bring to your own role in the stepfamily. This itself can create some anger or disbelief, for example, a child realising they are no longer the only girl or boy, or a visiting stepchild losing their special status as the 'baby' of the stepfamily.

Try and make life simple for yourselves in the first few weeks:

* get whatever extra help you can - from family, friends, neighbours
* don't try to be supermum or superdad!
* keep visits by others to your household short
* arrange for older siblings to have short visits away to give you a break as parents and them a break from the baby
* buy convenience foods if you can afford it
* make lists of essential tasks and arrange who will do them
* put aside non-essential tasks and don't feel guilty about them

There may be some stepfamilies where both adults and children find the baby's arrival far more disruptive than they could have imagined.

* Children may re-experience some of the feelings and reactions that remind them of the break-up of their previous family - rejection by a parent, fear of losing a parent, anger at someone else taking up the time and attention of a parent, actual changes like being moved out of a bedroom.

* A step-parent may suddenly find behaviour they had previously put up with in a stepchild now intolerable, and start to worry that the new baby will learn bad habits by copying.

* Visiting children may be seen as a burden and made to feel less welcome.

* Both parents may be tired and the mother may have some mild depression.

None of these will endear the new baby to their half-brothers and sisters who may tease, ignore, provoke or upset the baby.

NEW ROLES AND RESPONSIBILITIES

The pattern and structure of a stepfamily is important. It is good to draw a family tree and add the baby in so everyone can see who is who in the family, where they fit in, the different ages and birthdays, the balance of males and females, the variety of names and relationships.

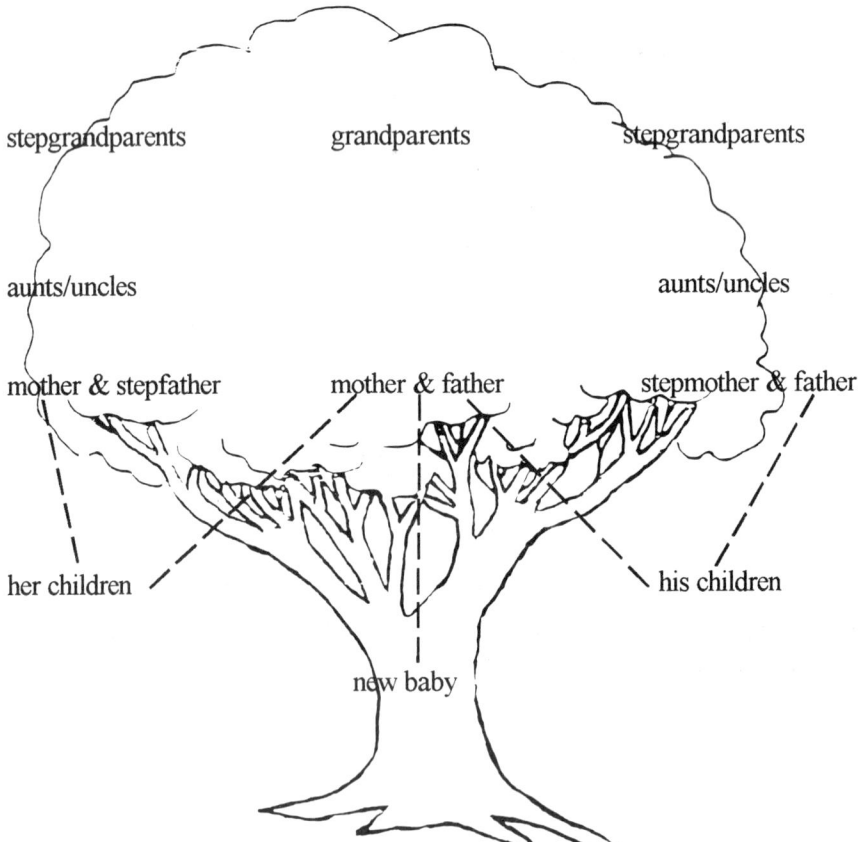

Working out your family tree - who is who in your stepfamily?

A child's place in their family is important to their sense of who they are. Overnight this can be changed when they become part of a stepfamily. Suddenly from being the eldest in one family they are the youngest in the stepfamily. An only child suddenly becomes one of four. The only girl or boy finds they have a rival in a step-brother or sister. A new baby is one more change in the pattern and structure of the stepfamily.

Adults' roles also change and many find the multiple parenting roles can become quite difficult. You and your partner are parents to the baby. You are a parent to your other children, but share their care with your ex-partner and with your new partner. And you may be a step-parent sharing the care of your stepchild with your partner who also shares the care of the child with their ex-partner. No wonder things are confusing at times and no-one knows who is in charge of making the decisions.

Everyone will also have brought patterns of behaviour learned from the past that may have hurt them - the death of a beloved parent, a bitter divorce, memories of tears and recriminations, arguments over money. There will also be lots of good memories and family traditions that can be woven together for the new stepfamily, combining good and bad, old and new.

Stepfather as father

If you are a full-time stepfather and a part-time father you may feel a mix of emotions. You may want to give this child all the love, attention and time you feel unable to give your other children because they live apart from you. You may feel guilty that you cannot share the baby with your children as easily as with your stepchildren. When your own children visit you may want them to have every chance to feed and play with the baby. If your stepchildren usually do this they may feel hurt and excluded and resent these 'visitors' who are allowed to take over. Equally, your children may feel this new baby is more important than them and may need time alone with you.

This dilemma can be avoided by explaining to all the children that the baby is to be shared and enjoyed by the whole stepfamily. As some of them are there all the time and some are only there occasionally, they will have to share looking after the baby according to who is available, with visitors having first option. If the children are old enough they can be encouraged to talk about how they feel with both parent and step-parent.

As a stepfather you may be surprised and even shocked at the strength of your feelings for your baby when you become a father. Do not be surprised if there is a contrast between your feelings for your child and your stepchildren. You may have thought you would feel no different after the birth of your own baby and be upset that you do.

You may think that because you love your own baby so much you may let your stepchildren down, or even 'short change' them on your love and attention. If you have been a caring considerate stepfather you are not likely to stop being one because you now have your own baby. What you are experiencing is felt by many stepmothers too, who love their stepchildren but in a different way to the way they love their birth children. Not better or worse, but different.

Stepmother as mother

As a mother of a new baby you may well experience similar problems to a father when it comes to sharing this child. You may be quite happy to allow your stepchildren to share some of the tasks and responsibilities of looking after the baby. On the other hand, you may be unable to come to terms with the fact that your new baby does not belong exclusively to you and your partner but already has a ready-made set of half-brothers and sisters.

As a stepmother looking after your stepchildren full-time, you may find it difficult and tiring also being a new mother with a tiny baby. If there have been difficulties with your stepchildren before the pregnancy and birth you may now have the added problem of the physical care of a newborn baby and the possible jealousy and additional misbehaviour of stepchildren.

> *Too much, too soon*
> *Jennie was a single woman of 36 when she married a divorced man with four children. They then had three children of their own quite quickly. When she contacted us for help she said that the root of their troubles lay in the first years of the marriage when she just could not cope with three tiny children*

and four older ones who needed a lot of understanding and love, as their mother had deserted them.

If you are likely to be in a similar position to Jennie it would be worth thinking about how you can arrange some extra help, not only when the baby arrives but over the next few years. Your health visitor may know of parent and toddler drop-in centres, local self-help groups, such as Parent Network, Meet a Mum Association (MAMA) or a STEPFAMILY group, where you could meet others coping with similar issues. National Childbirth Trust (NCT) post-natal support groups can be a life line and there might also be a befriending organisation, like Home Start, who could link you with a volunteer befriender to help look after the children and give you a break. The social services under eights officer may also be able to advise on day care provision.

Mother, stepmother and new mother

You may be one of the many women in a stepfamily who has three different sets of relationships with children in your family. There will be children of your previous relationship; your stepchildren; and children with your new partner. You will see the new baby develop from the time of birth as you did with your other birth children, whereas you will have known your stepchildren only from the time you first met. If, for any reason, you resented your stepchildren before the birth, then having the baby may only confirm the difference between your children and your stepchildren and how you feel about them. On the other hand, the new baby shares part of your stepchildren's parentage so you may be able to find similarities and shared characteristics which can help to form new bonds and feelings of belonging together.

Emotions and hormones do get stirred up during pregnancy and after childbirth. The five day 'blues' are a very common experience after the long wait for the baby and the excitement and activity of the birth. It is important to recognise your feelings in the early days and try and talk to someone about any anxieties you feel so that they do not disrupt or interfere with the bonding of all those in the stepfamily to whom the new baby is related in a way that no other family member is.

Children who have shown a lack of interest or even pretended anger at the thought of a new baby are usually won over when the baby arrives. Most children in any family have to cope with conflicting feelings of jealousy at the new arrival taking the time and attention of their parents and the novelty and wonder of this tiny creature who is their blood relation. For children gaining a half-brother or sister there may be competition to claim that he looks like them, or like their parent rather than their step-parent. What the new baby does signify, is that as a stepfamily they all belong in some way or another to each other and that can make a baby a very uniting and positive force in a stepfamily.

If you are a stepmother with stepchildren visiting rather than living with you all the time, this can be a challenge that often proves hard to meet. As a mother you may just have established a routine for the baby of feeding, bathing and sleeping, only to find all your work disrupted when your stepchildren visit for a weekend. It is only natural that stepchildren will want to see, play with and talk to this new half-brother or sister. Resentment can build up all too easily if visiting stepchildren feel they are being 'ordered' to keep away while the baby sleeps, or forbidden to take the baby for a walk, without an adequate explanation why. However small the visiting stepchildren are, they will understand and accept if they are told that the baby was awake half the night because he or she is teething, or that the baby can't go for a walk today because he or she has a temperature or it is too cold. It only takes a few minutes to give reasons for your answers and it is well worth the effort, no matter how tired or frustrated you may be yourself.

If you feel fiercely protective towards the baby, not wanting your stepchildren to have anything to do with the baby, but are quite happy for your own children to help look after and care for the baby, you may start to feel guilty and unhappy about such feelings. It may be hard for your partner to accept such rejection of his children and could seriously damage the relationship not only between you as a couple but between both of you and all the children. If this situation continues for long your stepchildren will begin to resent your attitude, and your own children may also become increasingly unhappy about their stepfamily life.

Such problems are best acknowledged as openly as possible. It may be overcome by talking through how you feel with your partner. You will probably be unhappy about the way you are behaving and need love and reassurance from your partner that there is nothing wrong with loving your own children so much. You should not feel guilty about not loving your stepchildren in the same way. However, it is important to find a way of living and being together that shows respect and awareness of the emotional needs of everyone in the stepfamily and you may need to seek help to achieve that.

Post-natal depression is quite common and many mothers still feel low six months after the birth. If such negative reactions towards any of the children or stepchildren continue, help should be sought quickly, either from the health visitor or family doctor. There are several organisations who can offer extra help and support at such times and it would be a good idea to get in touch with the local National Childbirth Trust group. It is essential that all those around offer practical and emotional support. A woman's self-confidence can be seriously undermined if she begins to doubt her own ability to be a mother.

Children and stepchildren

In any family most couples find they experience some problems with their first child when the second one arrives. An elder child can be very upset at no longer being the centre of attention. Jealousy, temper tantrums and misbehaviour are common problems and lots of love and reassurance are required from the parents to encourage love and care for the new brother or sister. There is always a danger of creating problems by looking for them and we would not want to suggest that problems are inevitable, only that they are normal!

> *Remembering the positives*
>
> *Sue wrote to our newsletter because of the negative images of stepfamily life being portrayed. She has three stepsons aged 11, 9 and 3 years old and daughters of 19 months and 3 months. Her priorities and those of her husband lie equally with all five of the children and she and her stepsons' mother*

have become good friends. None of her stepsons experienced any traumas after the births of their half-sisters. They all play together perfectly happily and the boys are protective of their little sisters.

Children in a stepfamily may react badly, however, if relationships between their parents are still in conflict, and especially if they were not told openly about the baby during the pregnancy. They, too, need to know that they are loved and wanted. This can sometimes be difficult if you have to deal with a rebellious adolescent stepchild who looks on your new partner not as a step-parent but as nothing more than the person who broke up their parents' marriage, or replaced their other parent. Or your own child may maintain absolute disgust at you having a child at your age, especially if their stepfather is younger than you, their mother.

Divided loyalties

Penny had been married before but had no children. Bob had two teenage children, both living with his ex-wife and visiting regularly. Bob had a demanding job and had played very little part in the upbringing of his two children. He and Penny agreed that with their new baby his children would be included in everything and asked to help with the baby as much as possible during visits.

Bob's daughter, aged 14, had eagerly awaited the birth and was ready to help out. Bob's son was older, 16 years. Although he seemed quite pleased about having a half-brother, Penny sensed that something was wrong. She was the one who noticed how rude and nasty her stepson had become if his sister showed too much attention to the baby.

She discussed her concern with Bob and they spoke to him together. Their problems were in part resolved when they

discovered that, up until the baby was born, Bob's son had always hoped that his parents would get back together again. When the baby arrived he knew that was no longer possible. He also resented his sister's love for the child and thought that, by showing her love for the new baby so openly, she was in some way betraying their mother.

When children in a stepfamily are unhappy, whether about a new baby or anything else, there are various ways of showing this. A general change of behaviour is usually an indication that something is wrong. Some of the more common examples are bedwetting in a toilet trained youngster, school age children may steal, become rude and insolent, refuse to eat meals with the family, not come straight home after school or stay out too late. This type of behaviour is very often present in other families when a new baby arrives or when the children feel they are being excluded, ignored or feel unloved for whatever reason. It is not confined to stepfamilies!

***Can history repeat itself?**
David was seven when a new baby joined his stepfamily. His stepmother thought both her stepson and her daughter had adapted well to the arrival of their half-sister. David's stepmother said she had problems dealing with him because he often went into great detail of how his mother did things differently for him. When David started to steal, however, it became obvious that this was a problem which needed sorting out. David was referred to a child psychiatrist who was able to explain to David's father and stepmother that the arrival of the new baby had disturbed David more than they had realised.*

David had confided to the psychiatrist that now the baby had arrived he was no longer needed in his family. David had got hold of the idea that since his father had left his mother, taking

him with him when he went, it was possible his father would now leave his stepmother, taking the new baby with him. By it's very existence, the baby presented a threat to David's stepfamily.

The history of the stepfamily and how it came to be formed, may play a crucial part in how children in a stepfamily react to a new baby. For all the children it is yet one more change and adjustment they are being asked to make because of the actions of one of their parents. The insecurity they may have felt at the time when their parents divorced, or when their parent died, may return. They may fear losing their remaining parent to the new baby or they may feel the baby took their other parent away.

The influence of the past on the present

Sue was ten years old when her father left her and her mother. She was old enough to hear the arguments about her father's 'other woman' but not old enough to understand exactly what was going on. Sue is now 15 years old. She says her mother was very distraught at being left and they came to rely on one another a great deal. It therefore took a lot of courage to tell her mother she wanted to see her father again and to meet his new family.

Sue now sees her father and stepmother every other weekend. Sue readily admits her dislike of her stepmother but is worried about the coldness and lack of feeling she has towards the older boy from her father's remarriage. She thinks it may be because the older boy is the result of her father's affair whilst he was still living with her mother. She absolutely adores the younger boy, whom she thinks of as her half-brother and cannot think of any other reason for feeling so differently about the older one.

If any of the children or stepchildren begin to show signs of jealousy or resentment to the new baby it will help if the parent and step-parent and all the children can discuss quite openly how they feel and what the other family members can do to help. It may be helpful to remind them all of how they felt before they became a stepfamily and how they now feel within the stepfamily.

Talking about the past can sometimes bring back painful memories. But, by looking at the past, each member of the stepfamily can begin to see why they may feel differently, perhaps because of the age they were when some events happened. It may also become clear why some members of the family feel more threatened or have particular kinds of problems.

If the problems persist do seek help and advice. You could ring the STEPFAMILY Helpline and the counsellor can help you talk through some of your anxieties and concerns and explore with you some options to address the issues. These may include contacting your health visitor or family doctor, seeing a family counsellor, joining a parent support group or asking for a meeting at your child and family guidance centre

A new baby for mother and for daughter
It is no longer uncommon for women in their forties and even some in their fifties to have a baby. Clearly this can mean that a couple who already have grown up children may have a child of this new relationship. Children often feel displaced when their parents start behaving as if they were young people again, or doing the same things as their children are now doing - forming relationships, setting up home, getting married and having children.

> ***Competition and embarrassment***
> *Ian and Marg both had grown up children who had left home when they met and fell in love. Their relationship developed to the stage were they moved in together and were very happy. Although they talked over their thoughts about having a baby with both sets of their adult children no-one really took them*

seriously. Certainly what no-one had considered was the possibility that Marg and her daughter would be pregnant at the same time. This proved an embarrassment to both when mother and daughter attended the same ante-natal clinic and classes. Neither Marg nor her daughter could explain why they felt so embarrassed, just that they did. They managed to cope with the odd stares they got from friends and neighbours and eventually were a great help to each other in the early months following the births.

Stepfamilies can begin to seem much more like the big old traditional families we hear so much about when there were lots of younger children around and the older ones could learn the realities of child care. There are likely to be more extended family members like grandparents, step-grandparents, aunts and uncles to turn to for help and advice. Whilst that may be true in part, a stepfamily is not the same since it is not all the same family but bits of different families coming together to form new stepfamilies. The history of stepfamilies is not always so easily or so readily told and family trees are important and invaluable in keeping track of who is who in each of the families you are related to.

Grandparents and grandchildren

Grandparents are sometimes the last people to be told, consulted or considered when a stepfamily is created. This is usually not because they do not matter, but because couples feel that their parents have been through enough worry or upset at the time of the divorce or death of their previous partner.

Grandparents sometimes have very strong views on the subject of their grandchildren. This may be especially so if, after a divorce or death, they took on the task of helping to look after the grandchildren and suddenly the grandchildren are whisked away to set up home with a step-parent.

Grandparents may be particularly concerned that when a new baby arrives, their grandchildren cannot possibly be having the same care and attention because the baby will be given priority. They may resent the fact that they are unable to offer the same help and support with the new baby as they had done before in the first marriage. This may be because they are now too far away, are physically unable to offer practical help, feel unwelcome, or it is inappropriate as their only link with the stepfamily is through the grandchildren. If it is their son who has remarried then the mother is likely to turn to her own parents who may have no interest in the step-grandchildren and are only concerned about their own new grandchild. If it is their ex-daughter-law who is having the baby then their involvement and interest may be misunderstood as intrusion.

It is often hard for grandparents to work out what is expected of them when their grandchildren's parents remarry.

> *A grandmother's pain*
> *One grandmother described how her grandson's father and stepmother will not let them take any treats or sweets for her grandson unless they take some for the stepmother's children too, who they insist are to be treated as step-grandchildren. She feels this is being unfair. After the death of their daughter her son-in-law was grateful for the help and support they were able to give and she used to see her grandson every day. Then the son-in-law remarried and she saw her grandson only rarely. Now that a new baby has arrived she anticipates that she will be expected to be very pleased and make a fuss, but she is adamant that she will not and that she just can't.*
>
> *'It is not that I do not want to love the new baby, it is just that I can't help feeling my grandson is being neglected. There are now three sets of children in that family, he is no longer the only child as he was when my daughter was alive. I am concerned about my grandson and I want to do the best for him. I am really not concerned about the others as they are really nothing to do with me.'*

The parents in this stepfamily are trying hard to establish the general family rule that all the children should be treated in the same way. The grandparents obviously find this hard to understand and accept. It is their only daughter's only child that they are concerned about and want to help but they feel powerless and angry. Perhaps the couple will be able to discuss this with the grandparents and allow the grandson to spend some time alone with them. It is just as important to let children retain the special relationship with their birth grandparents as it is to absorb the new extended family into the stepfamily.

> ***Frightened to love them in case you lose them***
>
> *Harry and Norma have a son who left his wife when their two children were of school age. Contact between the two parents is poor and since their ex-daughter-in-law has remarried she has allowed no contact with their grandsons at all. This has hurt them greatly but they have come to terms with it. When their own divorced daughter remarried, the elder grandson decided he did not like his stepfather and went to New Zealand to be with his own father and promised to keep in touch. Again, Harry and Norma were upset but had to accept it.*
>
> *Their daughter has just had another baby and Norma has found it very hard to take an interest in this new grandchild. Even at her granddaughter's christening she could not bring herself to hold the baby as she had the other grandchildren. It has been a shock for her daughter and new husband to find such a hard, cold response to the arrival of this new grandchild.*
>
> *Norma explained that she found it hard to admit both to herself and to her husband that she is frightened to love this baby in case she loses her. She loved the other grandchildren so much that when they moved away and she was unable to see them it almost broke her heart. She felt she had played an*

important part in the lives of all her grandchildren, often caring for them while their parents worked and got their homes together. She feels betrayed both by her children and the grandchildren whom she no longer sees. She can't bear the thought of losing another grandchild.

NEW FAMILIES, NEW BABIES, NEW HOPES

A new baby is a demonstration of our belief in the future. Where there is already a household of children, both full-time and visiting stepchildren, a new baby provides a direct link between them all. The baby is not a part of anyone's other family but of this new family where they all belong. In many stepfamilies a new baby unites everyone so that past jealousies or feuds are forgotten. For some teenagers in stepfamilies it may be easier to express love and show affection to a baby who turns to them so openly and trustingly than to a step-parent or stepbrother or sister.

However, we all know that all families can have difficult patches. Families and stepfamilies will have to cope with the hurly burly of day to day family life and the difficulties, conflict and misunderstandings that come their way along with the fun and good times. By describing some very different stepfamilies and how they tried to work things out, we hope you will realise that stepfamilies are very complicated places to live and you are not alone in finding it a struggle sometimes.

Stepfamilies, families, couples, parents and children - the most important thing is to keep the lines of communication open to everyone so that you can discuss any anxieties before they become big problems. It is difficult to write a booklet like this without it sounding as if everything will be fine as long as everyone behaves in a calm, civilised way and talks things through sensibly. This is not how it usually happens. People get hurt and offended by someone else's attitude. They become ill and miserable and downhearted when every day seems to bring a new problem or the same ones over and over again.

There are a lot of issues to come to terms with when a new baby is born. Tempers are sometimes lost, wrong or hurtful things get said in the heat of the moment. We are all human beings who are not perfect and most of us get very tired when a new baby is making demands twenty-fours a day.

Every couple hopes that their baby will bring with it the stability, unity and love that a family seeks. This is no less true in a stepfamily. Stepfamilies may have to work that little bit harder to achieve the desired results because there are so many extra people around with different expectations and concerns. But the rewards make it worthwhile.

We hope there will be many couples who have had none, or very few, of the difficulties discussed in this booklet. No couple in a stepfamily should assume they will have problems, or find it any harder to cope with their feelings after the birth just because they are a stepfamily.

For some stepfamilies the arrival of a new baby is the confirmation of the remarriage. For a step-parent who previously had no birth children it can bring a much deeper awareness and understanding of the joys and sorrows, the role and responsibilities of being a parent. Where the children have already grown up and left home the new couple will undoubtedly feel that this is their new family with a wealth of extended stepfamily relations that they and their child can value and enjoy over the years to come.

> ***Enriching all our lives***
> *Joe was on his own for a while with his three children after his wife died of cancer. He met Sally, who had two children, and since their marriage they have had a child of their own. It had not been easy for them to make the decision - having five children was already quite a handful and it was not easy on just one salary.*
>
> *Joe and Sally say the new baby has enriched their lives not only as a couple but also as a stepfamily. Joe's children have been*

able to ask questions about their own mother when they were little as well as enjoy their baby half-brother. Sally's children have also welcomed the new baby and their jealousy of their father's new baby in his new marriage has eased a little as they realise that both babies are part of their bigger family.

All the children seem more settled and secure in the stepfamily. The new baby has helped them open up some of the past, to make sense of the present and to look forward to the baby growing up and the future for them all.

Useful books

Very few baby and child care books have sections on preparing for a baby in a stepfamily although some mention is occasionally made in the more recent books. Remember that the impact of change on any child in a family can be disruptive and threatening and that is often what children in stepfamilies experience.

Do not assume that any problems you may encounter are because you are a stepfamily. It is more likely that being a stepfamily means you have to look at different ways of dealing with the situation and you may have to involve many other people to help you - such as the children's other parent, step-parent and grandparents.

Books for adults

The Childless Marriage (1985) Elaine Campbell, Tavistock

Coping with a Miscarriage (1980) Pizer and Palinski. Jill Norman

Get into shape after childbirth (1991) Gillian Fletcher. National Childbirth Trust

Pregnancy and childbirth (1986) Sheila Kitzinger. Penguin

*Stepmothering (1990) Donna Smith. Harvester/Wheatsheaf

*Step by Step, Focus on stepfamilies (1993) Margaret Robinson & Donna Smith. Harvester/Wheatsheaf

*Step-parenting (1988) Erica De'Ath. Family Doctor Publication

Stepping (1981) Nancy Thayer. Sphere. A novel about a young stepmother and her own new baby

The Blue Bedroom (1985) Rosamunde Pilcher, a short story - a stepchild, her stepmother and a new baby

The Parents Book, Getting on well with our children (1988) Ivan Sokolov & Deborah Hutton

> * Available direct from STEPFAMILY, 72 Willesden Lane, London NW6 7TA. Discounts for members.

Books for children

Mr Nobody's Eyes (1989) Michael Morpurgo, Heinemann. Ten year old Harry's widowed mother remarries and has a new baby.

Stepfamilies, What's happening (1991) Karen Bryant-Mole, Wayland.

The Growing Pains of Adrian Mole, and *The Diary of Adrian Mole, aged 13 $^{3}/_{4}$* (1982) Sue Townsend, Methuen - Mandarin

What Am I Doing In A Stepfamily? How two families can be better than one. (1982) Claire Berman. Picture storybook on divorce/death of parent, stepfamilies and brief mention of a new baby.

* A general list of books for children looking at the death, separation, divorce and remarriage of parents and being in a stepfamily is available from STEPFAMILY.

Useful addresses

Active Birth Movement,
55 Dartmouth Park Road,
London, NW5 1SL
tel 071 267 3006

CRY-SIS (support for parents with a crying baby)
BMCRY-Sis, London, WC1N 3XX
tel 071 404 5011

Exploring Parenthood
Latimer Education Centre,
194 Freston Road, London, W10 6TT
tel 081 960 1678

Foundation for the Study of Infant Deaths (CONI, Care of Next Infant Support) 35 Belgrave Square,
London, SW1X 8QB
tel 071 235 0965

Home-Start UK
2 Salisbury Road,
Leicester, LE1 7QR
tel 0533 554988

La Leche League
BM 3424, London, WC1N 3XX
tel 071 242 1278

Meet A Mum Association
58 Malden Avenue, South Norwood,
London, SE25 4HS
tel 081 656 7318

Miscarriage Association
c/o Clayton Hospital, Northgate,
Wakefield, WF1 3JS
tel 0924 200799

National Association for the Childless
318 Summer Lane,
Birmingham, B19 3RL
tel 021 359 4887

National Childbirth Trust (for breast-feeding and post-natal support)
Alexandra House, Oldham Terrace,
Acton, London, W3 6NH
tel 081 992 8637

National Stepfamily Association
72 Willesden Lane,
London NW6 7TA
tel 071 372 0844 (office)
    071 372 0846 (Helpline)

Parentline
Westbury House, 57 Hart Road,
Thundersley, Essex SS7 3PD
tel 0268 757077

Parent Network, (local support groups) 44-46 Caversham Road,
London, NW5 2DS
tel 071 485 8535

Strathclyde Stepfamily Association,
287 Dundyvan Road,
Coatbridge, ML5 4AU
tel 0236 436777

Working Mothers Association
77 Holloway Road London, N7 8JZ
tel 071 700 5771

Your local health clinic, health visitor, family doctor, family centre, social services under eights officer and the child and family guidance centre are all there to provide help, advice and support when you need it.

Don't be afraid to seek them out and ask for help. Check in your local telephone directory or with your local library, CAB or social services department.